Jump into Math

Active Learning for Preschool Children

Rae Pica

GH15757
A Gryphon House Book

The Learning in Leaps and Bounds Series

Jump into MATH

Active Learning for Preschool Children

Rae Pica

Gryphon House, Inc.
Beltsville, Maryland

© 2008 Rae Pica

Published by Gryphon House, Inc.

PO Box 207, Beltsville, MD 20704

800.638.0928; 301.595.9500; 301.595.0051 (fax)

Visit us on the web at www.gryphonhouse.com

Illustrations: Kathi Whelan Dery

Library of Congress Cataloging-in-Publication Data

Pica, Rae, 1953-

  Jump into math / by Rae Pica.

    p. cm.

  Includes bibliographical references.

  ISBN 978-0-87659-055-3

  1. Mathematics--Study and teaching (Elementary) I. Title.

  QA135.6.P53 2008

  372.7--dc22

                2007026493

Bulk purchase

Gryphon House books are available for special premiums and sales promotions as well as for fund-raising use. Special editions or book excerpts also can be created to specification. For details, contact the Director of Marketing at Gryphon House.

Disclaimer

Gryphon House, Inc. and the author cannot be held responsible for damage, mishap, or injury incurred during the use of or because of activities in this book. Appropriate and reasonable caution and adult supervision of children involved in activities and corresponding to the age and capability of each child involved, is recommended at all times. Do not leave children unattended at any time. Observe safety and caution at all times.

Gryphon House is a member of the Green Press Initiative, a nonprofit program dedicated to supporting publishers in their efforts to reduce their use of fiber-sourced forests. This book is made of 30% post-consumer waste. For further information, visit www.greenpressinitiative.org.

Table of Contents

OVER

Introduction

Not long ago, while attending a professional event, I overheard a math professor from a local university ask a preschool teacher if she did math with four-year-olds. "No," she told him. As soon as the preschool teacher walked away, I made a beeline for that professor and informed him that, of course, preschoolers "did" math. And I told him how!

As adults, we tend to think about mathematics in an "adult" way, meaning we're likely to conjure up memories of what math meant to us in our school days. Our memories of early childhood may not be as strong as those of later years, and so we remember such subjects as algebra, calculus, and standardized tests. For far too many of us, those memories elicit shudders of horror. Even if thoughts of math don't inspire an unwelcome trip down memory lane, we may associate math with budgets and checkbook balances— still not the most pleasant of associations.

The preschool teacher talking with the university professor was likely thinking about math in the adult way—perhaps because the professor taught at the college level. Although the preschool teacher wasn't doing calculus and trigonometry with the children, I am convinced that, despite her claims to the contrary, she "did" math with the young children in her classroom. For example, when the children in her classroom played with blocks and other manipulatives, they were "doing" math. When they stacked, sorted, and compared objects, they were doing math. When they measured ingredients for cooking or baking projects, they were experiencing math concepts. When they played with sand and water, set the table in the housekeeping center, or heard nursery rhymes and stories, such as "The Three Little Kittens" and "Goldilocks and the Three Bears," they were doing math again. Furthermore, because quantitative concepts are part of the language of mathematics, every time the preschoolers worked *together*, explored *big* and *little*, grouped objects, or made a line with someone first and someone last, they were doing math!

The moral of the story is that while math may be an abstract content area to adults, to children math is always present in tangible ways.

Mathematics in Early Childhood

Several mathematics concepts are developmentally appropriate to explore with young children. *Jump into Math* begins by exploring quantitative concepts such as *big, small, high,* and *low,* among others. While these may seem simplistic to adults, for children they are an important part of the language of mathematics and form the foundation for later mathematical learning related to size, position, and more. And because they also contribute to word comprehension, understanding of these concepts contributes to emergent literacy.

Just as children need to learn to recognize the letters of the alphabet, they must learn to recognize numerals. The activities in Chapter 2, Number Awareness & Recognition, help teach young children this important skill. Children also must hear numbers, learn to count, and eventually begin to realize that numbers are symbols that *represent* something. These skills are addressed in Chapter 3, Counting, One-to-One Correspondence, & Measurement.

Even geometry, which may have driven some of us to despair in high school, should be experienced in early childhood. The trick is to look at it in the "child" way rather than the "adult" way—just as we do everything else in early childhood education. Geometry in the early years is not about perpendicular bisectors and obtuse angles. Children experience angles, but only the kind they can make with blocks or with their elbows and knees. Children are introduced to lines—vertical, horizontal, diagonal, and crossed—but not to formal vocabulary about lines, such as the terms *perpendicular* or *parallel.* In addition, children explore basic shapes such as circles, squares, and triangles. Children's eventual comprehension of polygons and trapezoids begins with an understanding of and appreciation for the fundamentals.

At some point, young children begin to recognize patterns and perform simple computation. However, teaching these math concepts should not be handled in the adult way of writing figures and symbols on a chalkboard or piece of paper. Acting out the song "Roll Over" is a more developmentally appropriate and far less abstract computational example that allows children really to see that five minus one leaves four.

The Rationale for Active Learning in Mathematics

In this age of accountability and standardized testing, literacy and mathematics are the two content areas receiving the greatest emphasis. After all, the linguistic and logical/mathematical intelligences, as identified by Gardner (1993), are the two most valued intelligences in our society and are the basis for all standardized tests. As a result, teachers—even at the preschool and early elementary levels—are facing enormous pressure to use seatwork and worksheets to help children meet standards and pass tests. Many believe they no longer have time for active learning.

Despite the changing priorities of adults, children have not changed in the way they learn best. They are still experiential learners who retain more when they use multiple senses in the learning process (Fauth, 1990). They still need to experience concepts physically to fully understand them (including math concepts), and research has shown that movement is young children's preferred mode of learning.

Additionally, recent brain research confirms that the mind and body are not separate entities—that the functions of the body contribute to the functions of the mind. For example, physical activity increases the capacity of blood vessels (and possibly even their number), allowing for the delivery of oxygen, water, and glucose ("food") to the brain. This, of course, optimizes the brain's performance (Jensen, 2000).

Moreover, when allowed to do the kind of active learning involved in the previous example of "Roll Over," children *see*, *hear*, and *feel* the concept of subtraction, which makes it far more real to them than digits and symbols on a worksheet.

What Math, Movement, and Music Have in Common

At first it might seem the only thing these three content areas share is that they all begin with the letter "M." Sadly, only the first—math—is considered important in the current educational environment. Yet, movement and music are vital parts of children's learning. Just as math is associated with logical/mathematical intelligence (Gardner, 1993), movement and music are associated with their own intelligences (bodily/kinesthetic and musical, respectively). That means they are also valid ways of learning and knowing, which is just the beginning of what these three subjects have in common.

For example, anyone who has looked at a piece of sheet music has seen that fractions are part of both music and math. In music, a fraction represents a number related to beats. The number on top indicates the number of beats in a measure (a musical phrase), and the number on the bottom refers to the kind of note that equals one beat. For example, in music, a 2/4 meter means that there are two quarter notes to each measure. A quarter note is like a walking step, in that it takes about the same amount of time to complete. Polkas are performed in 2/4. So, the child happily moving to or accompanying a polka with a rhythm instrument or ribbon stick is getting the *feel* of a repeating 1–2. You can make that correlation between numbers and notes even more obvious by adding movement to the mix, for example by playing a game in which you clap and count along with the repeating 1–2. When the children are ready, they can sit and stamp their feet to the beat. Later, they can stand and stamp their feet. And, eventually, they will be able to move around the room matching the 2/4 beat of the music. All of these are experiences in counting, one-to-one correspondence, and patterning. And they are made more significant when they are experienced physically.

The musical element of pitch also can be connected to both math and movement. Pitch refers to the highness or lowness of notes. High and low are quantitative concepts that are also related to levels in space. Space is an element of movement. Children who move through the levels according to the highness or lowness of the pitches they are hearing are experiencing mathematical, musical, and movement concepts in ways that are long lasting and meaningful.

Similarly, *light* and *heavy,* two more quantitative concepts, can be explored with both the musical element of volume and the movement element of force. You can witness this when you play a piece of quiet music and invite the children to accompany it with the movements of their choice. It's not likely they will choose heavy, forceful motions; rather, the children are probably going to move lightly to it. By contrast, because loud music is unlikely to conjure up images of, say, butterflies, the children will probably move to it in more powerful ways. And if you give them an opportunity to experience the range from soft to loud and back again, the children also encounter the mathematical concept of a continuum.

There are other links, as well. Form in music is the overall design of the phrases, or musical ideas, that make up a song. "Row, Row, Row Your Boat," "Pop Goes the Weasel," and "Ring Around the Rosie" are in an AB form (there are only two musical phrases used in these songs). Because of its repeating final phrase, "Twinkle, Twinkle, Little Star" is in an ABA form. When children use the same movements for repeated phrases and different movements for contrasting phrases, they gain valuable experience with the mathematical concept of patterning.

Finally, a connection exists between math and the movement elements of time and shape (how quickly or slowly movements are performed, and the various shapes the body can assume while moving). Time is one of the cognitive concepts that contributes to "the gradual acquisition of math concepts" (Essa, 2003). When children move very slowly and very quickly—and at speeds in between—they begin to understand time. When they do it to the accompaniment of music at corresponding tempos, it becomes much less abstract to them. And shape, of course, is significant to geometry. When children take on the shapes of the previously mentioned circles, squares, and triangles using their bodies and the bodies of their friends, shapes, too, become much more real.

As you can see, therefore, math, movement, and music share much more than the letter "M." Using the three in combination offers children active, meaningful learning experiences.

How to Use This Book

The activities in *Jump into Math* offer children opportunities to experience physically and fully—through their bodies and/or their voices—mathematical principles such as quantitative concepts; number awareness and recognition; counting, measurement, and one-to-one correspondence; basic geometry; sequencing and patterning; and simple computation. These components make up the six main sections of this book.

Every activity in the book begins with information about how the activity supports mathematics as well as information to share with the children before starting. Next, the heading "To Have" lists any materials needed or advance preparation (most require no materials). "To Do" explains how to teach the activity. If an activity has extensions, they are listed under the heading "More to Do." When relevant children's literature or music is available, it is included along with an identifying icon—a book for literature and a musical note for recordings—to make them easy to identify. Use these suggested books and recordings to extend the children's learning.

The six sections of the book appear in developmental order, from least to most challenging. The activities within each section are organized according to their level of difficulty. However, the activities are not meant to be used one after the other, in the order in which they appear in the book. They do not progress in a

If you see this book icon,

the activity has a related children's book.

If you see this music icon,

the activity has related children's music.

neat, step-by-step sequence from point A to point Z because children do not learn in that manner. The six areas are interrelated, and children acquire knowledge in overlapping ways.

Begin with the simplest activities under Quantitative Concepts, repeating them as long as the children remain interested. (It is likely you will tire of them long before the children do, but that is okay; repetition is essential to reinforce learning in early childhood!) Skip—and mark—those extensions that are currently too challenging for the children. Then move on to the simplest activities under Number Awareness & Recognition. Continue in this way, letting the children alert you to when it is time to move on. (They should be experiencing at least an 80% success rate. When activities are too simple for them, they will become bored. When activities are too difficult for them, the children will become frustrated.)

When you have completed all the activities the children are capable of doing in each of the six sections, return to Quantitative Concepts. Repeat any activities you feel need reinforcing. For those with extensions, you should repeat the initial activity and then try the extension. If the children are not experiencing more success than failure when doing the extension activity, move on to Number Awareness & Recognition, repeating and extending as you see fit.

Whether you use these activities during circle or group time, substitute them for more "traditional" lessons in math, or use them as follow-ups to traditional lessons, you can be sure the children are moving in leaps and bounds toward understanding mathematics. Moreover, because you will have taught to the *whole child*—using all of the developmental domains—the physical, social/emotional, and cognitive—you can be sure the lessons learned will be long lasting and meaningful.

Chapter 1

Quantitative Concepts

Young children like to talk in terms of how *big* or *small* something is, whose train is the *longest*, or how many *more* toys they have than someone else. Without realizing it, they're dealing with an important part of the language of mathematics: quantitative concepts. Mayesky (2002) believes the following quantitative ideas should be part of the daily routines of young children. I've included as many as possible in this section of the book, all with the intention of promoting true understanding of them. Mayesky's list is as follows:

- big and little
- long and short
- high and low
- wide and narrow
- late and early
- first and last
- middle
- once
- few
- tall and short
- light and heavy
- together
- same length
- highest
- lowest
- longer than
- bunch
- group
- pair
- many
- more
- most
- twice

Follow the Leader

Follow the Leader is a fun and familiar game that can help reinforce the quantitative concepts of first, last, *and* in the middle.

To Have

No materials needed

To Do

- Lead the children around the room, performing whatever locomotor (traveling) skills they can all successfully execute. Be sure to use the words *first, last,* and *in the middle* to describe the children's positions.
- Vary your tempo (slow, fast, and in between); pathways (straight, curving, and zigzagging); force (light, strong, and in between), and levels (high, low, and in between).

More to Do

- When the children are ready for the responsibility, let them take turns leading.
- As you lead the group, occasionally call out the name of one of the children. That child breaks away from the line, leading everyone who's following. This will change the children's positions, which you should continue to point out.

Follow the Leader, written by Erica Silverman and illustrated by G. Brian Karas, makes a wonderful accompaniment to this activity.

Light vs. Heavy

Light and heavy *are two of the quantitative concepts Mayesky (2002) tells us children should experience daily. Because they are related to the movement element of force, they lend themselves easily to active learning.*

To Have

No materials needed

To Do

- Invite the children to sit and tap their fingers lightly on the floor in front of them. Next, ask them to pound their fists on the floor.
- Continue to alternate between the two, varying the amount of time they get to do each and pointing out the contrast between the light and heavy movements of the children's hands.

More to Do

- Ask the children to move as lightly as possible around the room. Encourage them to imagine that they are walking on eggs and trying not to break them.
- Next, invite them to move heavily, making as much noise with their feet as they can. Continue to alternate between the two.

"Hippo Is Heavy" is a children's favorite from Hap Palmer's *Animal Antics.* "Put Your Little Foot" from Kimbo's *Baby Face* calls for tiptoeing and stomping.

Rabbits & 'Roos

Children love to pretend to be animals. This activity, which gives them the opportunity to move like rabbits and kangaroos, offers additional experience with moving lightly and heavily. It also provides contrast between such other quantitative concepts as big *and* small *and* high *and* low.

To Have

No materials needed

To Do

- Talk to the children about rabbits and kangaroos. Ask them to tell you which of the two is bigger.
  - Which is smaller?
  - Which is heavier?
  - Which is lighter?
  - Which would move the most heavily?
- Then ask them to move first like one animal and then the other.
- Alternate between the two, using the words *small, light, big,* and *heavy* to describe what the children are doing. Also point out the low and high jumps.

rabbit & 'roo

light & heavy

"Rabbits & 'Roos" is an instrumental by Richard Gardzina, available in Rae Pica's *Moving & Learning Series: Preschoolers & Kindergartners.*

High & Low

This activity fosters understanding of the quantitative concepts of high *and* low, *while simultaneously promoting flexibility through stretching and bending. And because it is both an active listening and a body-parts experience, this simple activity also contributes to emergent literacy and science knowledge, respectively.*

To Have

Slide whistle (optional)

To Do

- Invite the children to show you how high they can make their hands go. How low can they go?
- Repeat, asking them to get their noses, elbows, belly buttons, and whole bodies as low and high as possible!

More to Do

- Using the slide whistle or your voice (humming or intoning), begin with a low note and move increasingly higher. When your voice is as high as it can go, reverse the process with descending notes. The children, meanwhile, start in squatting positions and rise and descend along with the notes.
- Repeat the process several times, varying the tempo.

You can find a recorded version of "High & Low" in all three of the books comprising Rae Pica's *Moving & Learning Series (Toddlers, Preschoolers & Kindergartners, and Early Elementary Children).* Also, Hap Palmer's *Learning Basic Skills, Volume 4: Vocabulary* includes a song called "High and Low."

Reinforces understanding of quantitative concepts related to force and weight

Light vs. Heavy II

Soft and loud music can help inspire the children to move in light and heavy ways, respectively. This activity also fosters understanding of the musical element of volume and the movement element of force.

To Have

Recordings of soft and loud music

To Do

- Play soft music and invite the children to tiptoe, move like a cat sneaking up on a bird, or "float."
- Then play loud music, suggesting that the children stamp their feet, swing their arms forcefully, or move like a dinosaur or elephant.
- Using the appropriate vocabulary to describe the light and heavy/strong movements you're seeing will help reinforce the children's understanding.

light & heavy

(a bird)   (an elephant)

Children's songs that offer a contrast between soft and loud volumes include "Soft and Loud" from Hap Palmer's *The Feel of Music* and "Play Soft, Play Loud" from Jill Gallina's *Rockin' Rhythm Band*. Also, "Moving Softly/Moving Loudly" is included in the three books comprising Rae Pica's *Moving & Learning Series* (*Toddlers, Preschoolers & Kindergartners,* and *Early Elementary Children*).

A Pair of...

This activity introduces children to the idea of a pair, *but because it begins with body part identification it also falls under the content area of science. Explain to the children that a pair means that there are two matching objects—like a pair of socks.*

To Have

No materials needed

To Do

- Ask the children to point to the pairs appearing on their bodies, as you call out the names of these parts. Possibilities include the following:

eyes	feet	arms
ears	knees	pointer fingers
hands	legs	nostrils
elbows	shoulders	

More to Do

- Challenge the children to move around the room looking for pairs. Possibilities include a pair of shoes or mittens in the coat room, a pair of markers at the white board, or a pair of plants on a windowsill.

There are many children's books that focus on the concept of pairs. Among them are *A Pair of Socks*, written by Stuart J. Murphy and illustrated by Lois Ehlert, and *A Pair of Red Clogs* by Masako Matsuno. Because the latter explores the concepts of shoes around the world, it's also relevant to social studies.

That's About the Size of It

This activity has the children exploring the quantitative concepts of big, little, long, short, high, and low. As a bonus, because physically experiencing these concepts promotes word comprehension, it also offers lessons in emergent literacy.

To Have

No materials needed

To Do

- Invite the children to demonstrate the following with their bodies:

big	tall	high	long
small	short	low	short

- Explain that while the shapes they're taking on may be similar, the words are slightly different. Discuss how.
- Repeat the activity, helping the children to make distinctions. For example, *big* could be depicted with arms out to the sides, while *tall* tends to be demonstrated with arms above the head. *Long* could be demonstrated while lying down!

More to Do

- Ask the children to pair up, with partners demonstrating the contrasting sets below. (Partner activities further explore the quantitative concept of *together*.)

big/small	high/low
tall/short	long/short

- Invite the pairs to show you such concepts as:

same length	shorter than	
longer than	taller than	higher than

- Once the children are experiencing success with the preceding activities, challenge them to discover quantitative opposites for themselves. For example, invite the children to show you a low shape. Then invite them to show you the opposite of a low shape, without telling them what it is.

Lorenz Books publishes *Sizes (Let's Look At),* for children 4–8.

Wide & Narrow

Wide *and* narrow *are quantitative concepts that are a bit more challenging for young children than, say,* big *and* little. *However, once they've taken part in these activities, they'll understand them well!*

To Have

Wide and narrow strips of paper to use for demonstration purposes

To Do

- Using the strips of paper (or, perhaps, a narrow door opening versus a wide one), show the children the difference between *wide* and *narrow*.
- Invite the children to show you *wide* and *narrow* shapes with their arms, fingers, legs, and whole bodies!

More to Do

- Ask the children to pair up, with one partner demonstrating a wide shape and the other a narrow shape. Then ask them to switch roles. Encourage them to try to come up with new shapes and not simply imitate their partners.

Wide & narrow

- Challenge the pairs to show you *wide* and *wider than.* (For example, one child stands with feet and arms somewhat apart, while the second child extends feet and arms to their fullest.)
- When the children have fully grasped this concept, ask them to form groups of three and to show you *wide, wider,* and *widest.*

A Few Good Kids

This simple activity reinforces the quantitative concepts of single, a pair, a few, *and* a group (*or* bunch).

To Have

Manipulatives to demonstrate the above-mentioned concepts

To Do

- With the children scattered throughout the room, explain that they're now demonstrating the concept of *single,* which means "alone." Then challenge them to work together to show you a *pair* (two), a *few* (a small number), and a *group* (or *bunch*), as you call out these words.

- Begin by repeating them in the same order every time, but eventually mix them up!

- You can also vary the tempo at which you call out the words. Remind the children, as necessary, of the meaning of each term.

Read *So Few of Me* by Peter H. Reynolds.

What Size Is It?

This activity in size comparison also serves as a lesson in suffixes.

To Have

No materials needed

To Do

- Invite the children to show you a big shape—but not too big (perhaps standing on tiptoe with arms raised overhead).
- Now challenge the children to make it a little bigger (perhaps by spreading arms wide) and, finally, the biggest it can be (spreading feet wide as well).
- Do the same with *little, littler, littlest* and *long, longer, longest.*

More to Do

- Working in trios, the children can together demonstrate concepts, such as *long/longer/longest, short/shorter/shortest,* or *wide/wider/widest.*

Tana Hoban's *Is It Larger? Is It Smaller?* is a photographic exploration of size.

Same Length

With this exploratory activity, the children gain experience with the quantitative concept of same length. *In addition, because it involves measuring and counting, it also provides practice with these other math concepts.*

To Have

No materials needed

To Do

- Invite the children to move around the room searching for objects that are the same length as (just as long as) their hands. How many can they find?

More to Do

- Challenge the children to find objects that are the same length as their arms, or the same length as the distance from their elbows to their wrists.
- The children will also enjoy discovering how many objects are longer or shorter than their hands, arms, or forearms.

 Part of the Math Counts series is *Length* by Henry Arthur Pluckrose.

Light & Heavy Words

This activity uses verbs that call for light or heavy movements. Because physically experiencing these words promotes word comprehension, emergent literacy is also promoted.

To Have

Words posted where the children can see them (optional)

Hand drum or tambourine (optional)

To Do

Alternate between "light" and "heavy" words, asking the children to demonstrate each. Possibilities for the former include *sway, tiptoe, stalk, float, glide,* and *melt;* for the latter, examples are *rock, stomp, stamp, pounce, crash,* or *explode.*

More to Do

- The above words lend themselves to depiction with the whole body, but you can also contrast words typically associated with the hands and/or arms alone. For example, "light" words could include *tap, pat, stroke,* and *flutter.* "Heavy" words might include *pound, poke, chop,* and *flap.*
- Use a hand drum or tambourine to signal changes from one kind of movement to the other. For instance, bang on the drum loudly to inspire stomping and tap on it lightly to inspire tiptoeing.

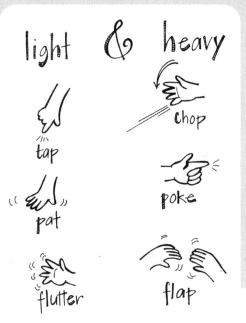

"Put Your Little Foot" from Kimbo's *Baby Face* calls for tiptoeing and stomping.

Once More, with Feeling

This activity explores the quantitative ideas of once, twice, *and* more.

To Have

No materials needed

To Do

- Ask the children to perform a simple movement, such as taking a step forward or lifting an arm. Explain that they've just done it once.
- Next, challenge the children to show you they can do it again, meaning they've done it twice. Can they do it once more? (They will have now performed the movement three times.)
- Ask the children to do two movements, such as stepping and clapping once, and then once more.
- If the children are ready, challenge them to do three movements, such as stepping, raising their arms above their heads, and clapping once, and then again, meaning they have performed the sequence twice.

Read *"More, More, More," Said the Baby,* by Vera B. Williams and *Bear Wants More* by Karma Wilson.

Equal & Unequal

Here the children discover the concepts of equal *and* unequal. *This activity also has some simple computation thrown in, and you can add counting to it as well.*

To Have

No materials needed

To Do

- Divide the children into two equal groups (if there are an uneven number of children, join the group to make it even) that stand facing other, with only inches between them.
- Invite each child to reach out and shake the hand of the person across from him or her, and explain that because everyone has a hand to shake, that means there's an *equal* (same) number of children.
- Have one pair at the end of the line move several steps away from the rest of the group and once again ask all of the children to shake the hand of the person opposite. There's still an equal number of children—both in the big group and with the partners.
- Now, ask one child from the big group to join the partners. Not everyone will have a hand to shake, because the two groups are now *unequal!*
- Continue in this manner, helping to foster understanding of the concepts.

More to Do

- With the children in two equal lines facing each other, have one line count off. **Note:** Children may need help to do this. The next line does the same. Explain that because each line reached the same number, that means there's an equal number of people in each line.
- Subtract one child from one line (who can stand with you and help with the counting) and have the two lines count off again. This time there will be an *unequal* number!
- You can also use activities like these to teach the concepts of *more* and *fewer.* When the lines are unequal, which line has more children? Which has fewer children?

Chapter 2

Number Awareness & Recognition

Copley (2000, p. 48) tells us that the "development of number concepts does not occur in one lesson, one unit, or even one year. It is a continuous process that provides the foundation for much of what is taught in mathematics."

Children begin counting from 1–10 long before these numbers have any real meaning for them, or before they are able to recognize the numerals—just as they begin reciting their ABCs long before they recognize letters on sight. The activities in this section promote visual recognition of numbers. They also begin to prepare children for writing numbers by familiarizing them with the straight and curving lines that compose the numerals.

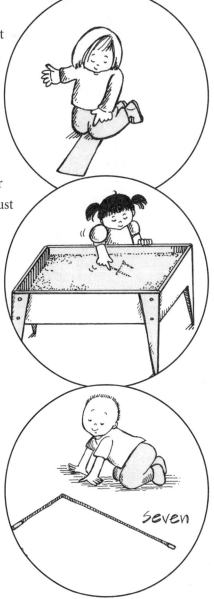

Promotes number identification

Beanbag Toss

This simple activity helps promote both number recognition and eye-hand coordination!

To Have

1 or more beanbags

Numbers 0–9, each on a large (at least 8½" x 11") card (at least one set of each number)

Note: If the concept of zero is too advanced for the children in your classroom, begin with the numeral 1.

To Do

- Scatter the number cards on the floor or ground in no particular order. Depending on the size of the area and the number of cards and beanbags available, invite one child (or more) at a time to stand at a designated spot and toss a beanbag onto a number. (To begin, the children should stand as close to the cards as necessary to ensure success.)
- When a beanbag lands on a card, call out its number.

More to Do

- Eventually, you can challenge the children to call out the number on which their beanbags land.

Among the many books that focus on numbers is *Numbers*, a board book by Michel Blake.

Matching Numbers

The children will love the social interaction involved in this game, and as they are playing it they will be learning to recognize numbers. The first version also reinforces the quantitative concept of pairs.

To Have

Numbers 0–9 on individual cards (two sets)

Note: If the concept of zero is too advanced for the children in your classroom, begin with using the numeral 1.

To Do

- Give one card to each child, who holds it at chest level facing outward. At your signal, the children begin walking around the room in search of a card that matches the one they are holding! Once children find a match, they continue walking side by side until all the matches are paired.

More to Do

- Once the children are all in pairs you can organize a number "parade" by putting the pairs in sequential order and having children march around the room holding their cards in the air.
- When the children are ready, invite them to organize the parade themselves!
- Use more than two sets of numbers, requiring the children to keep looking until they find all of the numbers that match their own.

Reinforces multiple numerical concepts

Hopscotch

This traditional game provides practice with number recognition, counting, and sequencing!

BEANBAG
(SKIP)

FOOT ON
NUMBER

To Have

Chalk

Flat, paved ground

Beanbag

Numbered carpet squares (optional)

To Do

● With chalk, draw one or more hopscotch grids on the playground surface or a sidewalk (10 squares, numbered consecutively, with the numbers 1, 2, 5, and 8 in single squares and the numbers 3 and 4, 6 and 7, and 9 and 10 in side-by-side squares).

● The children line up single file and the first child tosses a beanbag (whatever you've designated) onto the square marked with the numeral 1. The child then hops over that square (when possible, there should be no touching down on the square with the beanbag on it), lands on one foot in the square marked 2, jumps in the squares marked 3 and 4 (a two-footed landing with the left foot in the left square and the right foot in the right square), hops (one-footed landing) in the square marked 5, and so on up the grid. At the top of the grid, the child turns and follows the same pattern back to the beginning, once again hopping over the first square.

● The second child then tosses the beanbag into the square marked 2, and the process continues.

More to Do

● You can play this game indoors by using numbered carpet squares. But whether you play it indoors or out, as the children begin to excel at this game, make it more challenging by encouraging them to perform it at a faster tempo!

● To reinforce number recognition, the children should eventually say the number aloud as they move onto each square.

Share *Let's Play Hopscotch* by Sarah Hughes with the children.

Skywriting

When there is no permanent product (such as numbers written on a page) to demonstrate whether they've gotten it right or wrong, the children feel a lot less pressure. Besides, pretending to write in the air is fun!

To Have

Ribbon wands or chiffon scarves (optional)

Numbers 0–9, posted where the children can easily see them (optional)

Note: If the concept of zero is too advanced for the children in your classroom, begin with the numeral 1.

To Do

- Post the numbers, if available, for the children to reference.
- Ask the children to imagine that the air in front of them is a giant chalkboard and they've got a big piece of chalk—in any color they choose—in their writing hands.
- Invite them to choose any numbers they want and to "write" them on the "chalkboard." They should begin by making their numbers as large as they possibly can.

More to Do

- Encourage the children to gradually reduce the size of the numbers they make.
- Have one child at a time write a number in the air, with the rest of the class trying to guess which number it is.
- Invite the children to write with other body parts—an elbow, the nose, the top of the head, or the belly button. They absolutely adore this activity, particularly the belly button challenge!
- If you have chiffon scarves or ribbon wands available, using them as "chalk" makes the pathways in the air less abstract, and the children love these props.
- Ask the children to imagine that the floor in front of them is a big piece of paper and they have chalk, paint, or ink—in any color they want—on the big toe of one foot. The children use their toes to "write" any letters they want, in lowercase or uppercase, on the floor.

Straight & Curvy

This exercise in number recognition reinforces the idea that straight and curving lines comprise numerals.

To Have

Numbers 0–9, posted where the children can see them easily

Note: If the concept of zero is too advanced for the children in your classroom, begin with the numeral 1.

To Do

- Show the children that some numbers have straight lines, some have curvy lines, and some have both!
- Point to a number (those with the fewest lines—like 0, 1, and 7—are the easiest to reproduce) and ask the children to make it with their bodies or body parts.
- Repeat with several numbers.

More to Do

- When the children are ready for more challenging numerals such as 3 and 5, and for the greater challenge of working cooperatively, ask them to create numbers in pairs and trios.

 DK Publishing offers *My First Number Book.*

Reinforces number identification and introduces geometry concepts

All About Numbers

Here's another activity to promote number recognition! This one, however, has an additional benefit in that it also offers practice with lines and positional concepts, which are part of early geometry.

To Have

Large, cut-out numbers scattered around the floor

To Do

- Challenge the children to do the following:
  - Kneel on top of a number that has only straight lines.
  - Sit next to a number that has only curving lines.
  - Stand behind a number that has both straight and curving lines.
- When the children reach their destinations, they should tell you what the number is.

More to Do

- When the children are more skilled at number recognition, you can simply ask them to find specific numbers. When they reach the designated number, they take on its shape with their bodies.
- More challenging still is to ask the children to find the number that comes between, for example, 3 and 5.

Rebecca Emberley's *My Numbers/Mis Numeros* is a board book with colorful illustrations of numerals, which are identified in both English and Spanish.

Number Hunt

This "treasure" hunt requires that children recognize the numbers 0–9.

To Have

Numbers 0–9 on large, individual cards (at least one set of each)

Numbers 0–9, posted for the children to see

Note: If the concept of zero is too advanced for the children in your classroom, begin with the numeral 1.

To Do

- Beforehand, hide the number cards throughout the room—some in easy-to-find spots, and others in more challenging locations.
- Tell the children they're going on a treasure hunt for the numbers. (Point out the numbers you have posted so the children know what they're looking for.)
- As they find the numbers, the children should bring them to the center of the room.

More to Do

- When the children are ready to do so, once they've brought the found cards to the center of the room, invite them to arrange them in numerical order.

Carved in Sand

This activity uses the sense of touch, along with movement, to promote awareness of the number shapes. The results will be more tangible for the children than they were with Skywriting, allowing them to see their finished products. However, because the numbers are written in sand rather than on paper, the children should still feel less pressure to get them just right.

To Have

Sand (at a sand table, in a sandbox, or simply in a large box-like container)

Numbers 0–9, posted or on sheets

Note: If the concept of zero is too advanced for the children in your classroom, begin with the numeral 1.

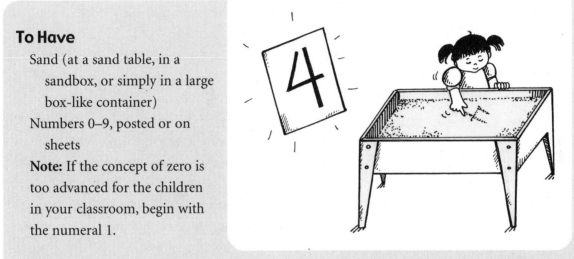

To Do

- Point to a number and invite the children to copy it in the sand with their pointer fingers.
- They then erase it with a hand and start the process anew with another number!

More to Do

- Once the children have experienced writing in sand with their pointer fingers they can try it with the handle of a wooden spoon. This helps promote fine-motor coordination while simultaneously helping accustom them to the feel of a writing implement. That makes this activity an exercise in emergent literacy, as well as mathematics.

Tracing Numbers

This activity imprints the shapes of the various numbers on the children's minds and bodies by asking them to form and then "trace" them. It also provides practice with locomotor (traveling) skills.

To Have

The numbers 0–9, posted where the children can see them

1 jump rope per child

Note: If the concept of zero is too advanced for the children in your classroom, begin with the numeral 1.

To Do

- Beginning with the numerals with the simplest shapes (0, 1, and 7), choose a number and ask the children to each make that number on the floor with the rope.
- Once a number is ready, invite the children to trace (move along) its shape with a locomotor skill of your choice (walking, jogging, and jumping are the easiest).

zero →

← JUMP ROPE →

seven

Chapter 3

Counting, One-to-One Correspondence, & Measurement

Children are counting long before it has any meaning to them—before they realize that the numbers *represent* something. As a result of rote memorization, children often are able to recite the sequence of numbers before the age of three. One-to-one correspondence—attaching a number to each object counted—comes much later and must be modeled. Preschoolers can mark objects as they count them; however, they have trouble keeping track of what they have and have not counted. Kindergartners can usually count at least five objects accurately, eventually learning to count six or more items by touching each item as they count (Copley, 2000).

According to Charlesworth and Lind (2003), one-to-one correspondence is "the most fundamental component of the concept of number." This section begins with rote counting, reinforcing the sequence of numbers, and moves on to counting steps taken, children, bubbles popped, and more, all of which promotes one-to-one correspondence.

Eventually, children use the skills they have acquired to learn about measurement.

Blast Off

This simple activity involves counting backward, but it's appropriate for even the youngest children and can help them advance from rote memorization of numbers to actual comprehension. Because the activity encourages the children to move from low to high positions, it provides experience with those quantitative concepts.

To Have

No materials needed

To Do

● The children squat low, pretending to be spaceships on their launching pads.

● Count backward dramatically from 10 to 1.

● When you say, "Blast off!" the children "launch" themselves upward. Repeat as long as the children stay interested!

Accompany this activity with *Blast Off! A Space Counting Book,* written by Norma Cole and illustrated by Marshall Peck.

Body Parts

This activity matches numbers to body parts, meaning the children don't have to count any higher than 10. Because it requires the children to identify body parts, the activity also falls under the content area of science.

To Have

No materials needed

To Do

- Invite the children to discover and point out the body parts that they have two of (eyes, ears, hands, feet, knees, elbows, eyebrows, and so on). How many body parts can they name? Which parts of the face come only in ones? (Possible answers include the mouth, nose, forehead, and chin.) How many fingers do they have? What else do they have 10 of?

 "The Body Poem," on the CD titled *Wiggle, Giggle, & Shake* by Rae Pica and Richard Gardzina also requires children to match numbers to body parts, this time counting no higher than four.

Promotes awareness of numbers in sequence

One, Two, Buckle My Shoe

Acting out this nursery rhyme reinforces the sequence of numbers from 1–10 and promotes emergent literacy.

To Have

Nursery rhyme, posted (optional)

Numbers 1–10, posted

To Do

- Read the nursery rhyme aloud while pointing to each number as it appears in the rhyme.
- Then read it again, more slowly, with the children acting out the lines.
- The nursery rhyme follows, with the actions below each line in brackets.

One, two, buckle my shoe; (Children pretend to fasten shoes.)

Three, four, shut the door; (Children pretend to shut a door.)

Five, six, pick up sticks; (Children pick up imaginary sticks from floor.)

Seven, eight, lay them straight; (Children pretend to draw straight lines on floor.)

Nine, ten, a big fat hen. (Children put hands under arms and cluck!)

Reinforce number awareness and counting with Keith Baker's *Big Fat Hen*, a colorful board book based on this nursery rhyme.

Musical versions of this nursery rhyme are available on Greg & Steve's *We All Live Together, Volume 3* and Hap Palmer's *Early Childhood Classics.*

One Little, Two Little

This musical activity reinforces counting and one-to-one correspondence and introduces the concept of sequence. You can also use it as a transition activity when dismissing children from group time to free time.

To Have

No materials needed

To Do

- With the children standing side by side in a line, point to one child at a time as you sing the following words to the tune of "Bumping Up and Down in My Little Red Wagon."
- When you point to each child, she or he steps forward from the line. (Remember to sing slowly.)

  One little, two little, three little children,
  Four little, five little, six little children,
  Seven little, eight little, nine little children,
  Now have left the line.

- Continue in this manner until you count all of the children.

seven...eight...nine

four...five...six

One, Two, Choo, Choo, Choo

Children love to play choo-choo train games. When they play this version, they reinforce counting skills.

To Have

No materials needed

To Do

- The children stand scattered around the room.
- Explain that you're going to make a train. Tell the children that you will be the engine, and that you will pick up one "car" at a time.
- Begin moving around the room. As each child hooks on (by placing hands on the hips of the last person on the train), call out the appropriate number. (When the first child hooks on, call out "one." When the second child hooks on, call out "two.")
- Once the train is complete, invite the children to tell you how many cars the train has.
- Move around the room for a while and then begin dropping off "cars" one at a time, once again calling out the corresponding numbers.

Red Train, written by
Will Grace and illustrated by Ed Vere, involves counting colorful trains.

44

Step Forward

This activity encourages the children to first recognize a number and then to count that number of steps. Be sure the children can count to 10 before choosing this game.

To Have

Numbers 1–10 written on individual cards

To Do

- The children line up side by side at one end of the room.
- Stand facing them at the opposite end and hold up one of the cards for them to see (it is best to start with low numbers).
- The children then take that number of steps toward you, counting aloud as they walk.

More to Do

- To give the children an opportunity to practice other locomotor skills, replace the steps with jumps, hops, gallops, or leaps.

Ray Heatherton's *Musical Adventures in Learning: All About Numbers and Counting* teaches the names of numbers and their correct order.

Reinforces counting and awareness of one-to-one correspondence

How Many Steps?

Counting begins to go from rote memorization to an understanding of one-to-one correspondence when the children have something fun to count. This activity stimulates their natural curiosity, which gives them a reason to count!

To Have

No materials needed

To Do

- Help the children line up side by side on one end of the room.
- Invite them to see how many steps it takes to get to the other side.
- Encourage the children to count aloud as they go, but quietly so that they do not interfere with other children's counting.

More to Do

- You can use this activity anywhere—counting the number of steps it takes to cross the playground, to circle the room, or to move down the hall and out the door. The latter is a great transition activity!
- Use this as an opportunity to practice other motor skills. Instead of steps, invite the children to discover how many jumps or hops it takes to get from one place to another.

One, two, three, four, five, six, seven...

 Among the many counting books are *Counting Crocodiles* by Judy Sierra and *Anno's Counting Book* by Mitsumasa Anno.

Pop & Count

Chasing bubbles promotes cardiovascular endurance (running) and muscular strength and endurance (jumping), but when you add counting to the mix, it becomes a mathematics experience!

To Have

A bottle of bubble solution with a wand

To Do

- Blow bubbles for the children to chase and pop.
- Each time a child pops one, he counts it, with each child increasing the previous number by one. For example, if Keesha pops the first bubble, she calls out "one." If Marco pops the second bubble, he calls out "two."
- The rule is that no child is allowed to pop two bubbles in a row.
- When the children reach numbers that are too high for them to count, you can help them.

Pop! A Book about Bubbles, written by Kimberly Brubaker Bradley and illustrated by Margaret Miller, makes a fun accompaniment to this activity.

Reinforces counting and one-to-one correspondence

Count the Claps

Because this is an active listening experience, it falls under the heading of language arts as well as mathematics.

To Have

No materials needed

To Do

- Sit with the children and, without counting aloud, clap your hands a certain number of times (starting with low numbers).
- The children then clap out the same number of claps, counting aloud as they do.

Clap Your Hands by Lorinda Bryan Cauley invites children to perform a variety of actions.

Body Jive by Ambrose Brazelton encourages children to move in many different ways.

Treasure Hunt

What child doesn't love a treasure hunt? Counting found objects makes it a math experience.

To Have

Several items with a unifying theme (for example, stuffed animals, plastic eggs, or farm animals)

Basket or tote bag for each child

To Do

- Beforehand, hide the items throughout the room.
- Tell the children what you've hidden, and then let them go in search of them! When a predetermined amount of time has passed (say, five minutes), bring the children back to the center of the room, where they empty the contents of their bags and count their own items.
- Put all of the items together and invite the children to count them as a whole.

More to Do

- To get the children out into the fresh air and sunshine—and to make this a science experience—hold your treasure hunt outdoors with natural materials. For example, challenge the children to find as many rocks, or fallen leaves, as they can.

Counting, One-to-One Correspondence, & Measurement   49

Reinforces counting, one-to-one correspondence, and the quantitative concept of how many

How Many Feet?

Children enjoy the fun involved in this counting activity. Also be prepared to count giggles!

To Have

2–3 carpet squares or plastic hoops

To Do

- Place a carpet square or hoop on the floor and ask the children to sit around it. (If the children don't fit comfortably around one, add more squares or hoops.)
- Invite them to discover—and count—how many of their feet can fit on the square or inside the hoop.

More to Do

- When the children are familiar with this activity and are ready to respect one another's personal space, you can try this activity with the children standing.
- Challenge the children to discover how many hands fit on the square or inside the hoop. This will require bending, so it will promote flexibility, one of the five health-related fitness factors.

Hold That Statue

Children love the traditional statue game. This version adds the elements of counting and measuring time to the game.

To Have

Music

Tape or CD player

To Do

- Invite the children to move while the music is playing and to freeze like statues when it stops (you press the pause button).
- While they remain still, count aloud the number of seconds they must stand like statues. Each time you stop the music, vary the length of time before you restart it.
- When the game is over, ask the children if they remember the longest time that they had to be statues.

More to Do

- When the children understand how this works, invite them to count the seconds themselves.

Counting, One-to-One Correspondence, & Measurement

Reinforces counting and one-to-one correspondence

Three-Legged Creatures

This game offers children a fun way to practice counting. And, because it involves cooperation, it also falls under the heading of social studies.

To Have

1 long scarf for every 2 children

To Do

● With the children paired up and standing side by side, gently tie their inside legs together with the scarf.

● Challenge the children to count how many steps they can take in a predetermined amount of time, then give them the signal to go!

More to Do

● Give the children opportunities to practice other locomotor skills by inviting them to perform on three legs the skills they're able to perform alone. Possibilities include jumping (in this case, on three feet), hopping (on two feet, lifting either the inside or outside legs), and galloping (with either the inside or outside feet leading).

Time's Up

This game offers children experiences with counting and the concept of time. And because it's cooperative, it also falls under the content area of social studies.

To Have

1 parachute
Several small, soft balls
Timer

To Do

- Gather the children around the parachute and place the balls on top of it.
- Explain that the challenge is to lift the parachute and make ripples with it (move it lightly up and down) while keeping the balls from falling off!
- Set the timer. At your signal, the children begin, counting the number of times they lift the parachute.
- When the time is up (say, 30 seconds, to begin with), the children tell how many times they were able to lift the parachute without losing any of the balls. (If any balls fall off before the timer goes off, reset the timer and start again.)
- Each time you play this game, set the timer for a little longer!

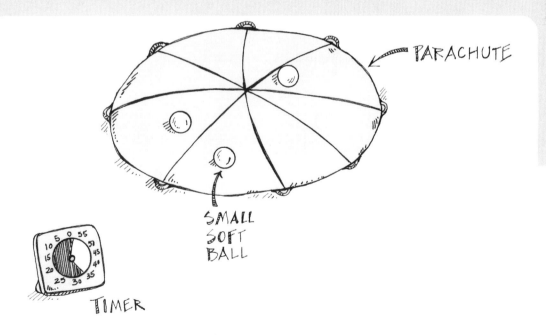

PARACHUTE

SMALL
SOFT
BALL

TIMER

Reinforces counting and quantitative concepts

Simon Says

Because it involves active listening and counting, this version of Simon Says is both a language arts and a mathematics experience.

To Have

No materials needed

To Do

- "Simon" challenges the children to perform a certain number of actions. For example:
  - clap two times
  - take three steps
  - jump once
  - count to five
  - blink twice

- If you arrange the children in two lines or circles, a child who moves without Simon's "permission" simply goes from one line or circle to the other. This allows for continuous participation and opportunities to learn and succeed!

There are musical versions of Simon Says on Frank Leto's *Move Your Dancing Feet* and Greg & Steve's *We All Live Together, Volume 3.*

Mother, May I?

This modified version of an old game, excerpted from Great Games for Young Children *(Pica, 2006), allows all of the children to participate simultaneously—and to practice their counting skills!*

To Have

No materials needed

To Do

- Acting as "Mother," stand facing the children, about 20 feet away.
- Give an instruction for the children to take a certain number of a certain kind of movement, for example, "Children, take five steps on tiptoe" or "Children, take three jumps backward."
- The children then ask, "Mother, may I?" before doing as directed.
- The game continues until the children reach you. You can then start all over again!

More to Do

- When the children understand the game, invite them to take turns acting as Mother.

Reinforces counting and awareness of time

How Long Does It Take?

This activity takes advantage of the innate curiosity that causes children to want to figure things out. What they'll be figuring out here, through counting, is the measurement of time.

To Have

1 chiffon scarf (or paper towel square) per child

To Do

- Invite each child to toss her or his scarf into the air and to count aloud to determine how long it takes for the scarf to float down to the floor.

- Encourage the children to try it several times. Does it always take the same amount of time? Does it make a difference if they toss the scarf higher?

More to Do

- Suggest that the children try this same experiment with both a lightweight ball (such as a beach ball or a foam ball) and a heavy ball (such as a playground ball). Which of the three items—the scarf, the lightweight ball, or the heavy ball—comes down the fastest/slowest? Why?

How Many Claps?

Similar to the previous activity, this one uses even more senses to help children count and measure time.

To Have

1 small, soft foam ball for each child

To Do

- Spread the children throughout the room or playground.
- Give each child a ball.
- Ask the children to throw their balls into the air and see how many times they can clap before they come back down to the ground.
- They should count aloud as they clap.

More to Do

- When the children are developmentally ready to catch, they can do the same activity but this time counting how many times they can clap before catching the ball.

Reinforces counting and one-to-one correspondence

How Many Parts?

With an activity like this, it's easy to determine which children may be having trouble with counting. However, because children think differently than we do, we first have to determine how they're counting before we decide if they understand the concept. For example, some children will count the foot as five body parts.

To Have

No materials needed

To Do

● Invite the children to place a certain number of body parts on the floor. (Only that number of parts should be touching the floor.)

● Then move around the room, counting the parts aloud and pointing out all the different possibilities they discovered.

● Repeat the activity several times, varying the number of body parts and challenging the children to use the same number but different parts. For instance, a challenge to touch the floor with three body parts could result in two feet and a hand, two knees and an elbow, and so on.

More to Do

● Challenge the children to count how long they can hold very still in each position!

Hold That Balance

This cooperative activity involves balance, which puts it under the headings of both social studies and science. Math comes into play as the children count to measure time.

To Have

No materials needed

To Do

- Standing in a circle, the children each place their hands on the shoulders of the children on either side of them.
- Ask the children to rise onto their tiptoes and count the number of seconds they can remain still.
- Try this several times. Do they always get to the same number? What was the lowest? The highest?

More to Do

- Change the contact from hands on shoulders to hands held or arms around one another's waists.
- Ask the children to rise onto their tiptoes and then lower their heels in a specific number of seconds, which you count aloud. For example, as you count out four seconds, they lift their heels. Count out another four seconds, during which they hold still. And during the final four seconds, they lower their heels. The higher the number and the more slowly you count, the more challenging it will be.

HEELS OFF the FLOOR

- Make the balances more challenging by asking the children to stand on one foot, to extend one leg into the center or to the outside of the circle, or to lean forward or backward. All of these can be performed either flat footed or on tiptoe.

Reinforces counting and problem-solving abilities

How Many Ways?

This activity requires the children to do some investigative thinking as they count!

To Have

No materials needed

To Do

- Choose a body part—a hand, for example—and ask the children to discover how many ways they can move it.
- Repeat with other body parts, including an arm, a leg, the head, or a foot.

"How Many Ways?" is the name of one of the songs on Hap Palmer's *Math Readiness*.

How Many Ways? II

This variation on the previous activity gives children the opportunity to explore, count, and discover while also practicing a variety of nonlocomotor skills.

To Have

1 crayon and piece of paper per child

To Do

- Choose a nonlocomotor skill, such as stretching, bending, turning, shaking, or swinging from side to side.
- Invite the children to perform the skill once in any way they want.
- Challenge them to discover how many different ways they can perform that same skill. (If they need a bit of help, you can encourage them to try at different levels and in different directions. For example, if a child first stretches toward the ceiling, he or she might then stretch forward. If a child turns first toward the right, she or he might then try it in toward the left.)
- Show the children how to make tally marks on their papers to keep track of all of the different ways of moving that they discover.
- Ask the children to count the tally marks and then compare the numbers.

How Many Parts? II

This activity, adapted from Wiggle, Giggle, & Shake *(Pica, 2001) invites the children to discover the number of body parts that can perform a variety of nonlocomotor skills.*

To Have

1 piece of paper and crayon per child (optional)

To Do

- Ask the children to show you how the whole body performs the following nonlocomotor skills: shaking, bending, stretching, twisting, and swinging.
- Then, focusing on one skill at a time, ask the children to find how many body parts can also perform them. For example, it's possible to shake a hand, an arm, a leg, the head, and the hips.
- Show the children how to make and tally slash marks for the parts discovered.

More to Do

- Invite the children to discover if the number of body parts changes if they move from a standing to a kneeling to a sitting to a lying position.

Promotes counting and problem-solving skills

How Many Sounds?

Like the last activity, this one requires investigation along with counting.

To Have

1 8½ x 11 sheet of paper

To Do

- Pass around a sheet of paper, inviting each of the children to make a different sound with it.

- The children should count aloud consecutively with each new sound discovered. Possibilities include tearing, flicking, crumpling, smoothing, and folding it.

- Help them find new ideas by suggesting they use body parts other than their hands. Possibilities include rubbing it on their heads, blowing across it, smashing it underfoot, and rolling it up and using it as a horn.

Counting, One-to-One Correspondence, & Measurement 63

Reinforces counting, one-to-one correspondence, and problem solving

It Takes Two

With this game, the children discover how many ways they can move when a certain restriction is imposed. Because it's a cooperative activity it also falls under the content area of social studies.

To Have

No materials needed

To Do

- Invite pairs of children to connect various body parts—one set at a time—and to count how many different ways they can find to move without breaking the connection. (Encourage the children to count aloud as they discover new possibilities.)
- When they've run out of possibilities, challenge them to try another set of body parts. Connections might include the following:
  - right (left) hands
  - both hands
  - right (left) elbows
  - both elbows
  - one or both knees
  - right (left) feet
  - backs

More to Do

- Suggest nonmatching body parts, like a hand to an elbow, a hand to the back, or a wrist to a shoulder.

How Many Hands?

Measuring with rulers and tape measures may be something children have seen adults do. But, for them, it has no real meaning. This activity asks them to measure with their hands, which is far less abstract!

To Have

No materials needed

To Do

- Invite the children to sit scattered on the floor.
- Ask them to place one hand at the tops of their knees.
- "Walking" their hands alternately down their legs, how many hands is it from the knee to the toes? (You will likely have to demonstrate this for them.)
- How many hands is it from the hip to the toes?

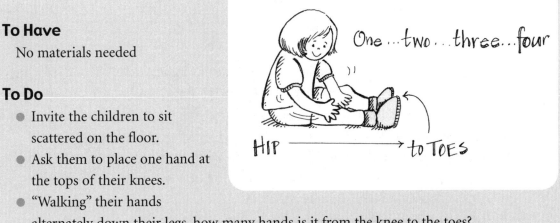

One...two...three...four

HIP ⟶ to TOES

More to Do

- Help the children group themselves into pairs. Encourage one child in each pair to lie face up on the floor, while the other child walks her hands next to her partner's body from toes to head to measure his height.
- Invite the children to measure anything in the room this way.

How Far?

This is a fun introduction to measuring with yardsticks.

To Have

1 yardstick per child

To Do

- Arrange the children in a side-by-side line against a wall (if you have too many children to afford enough space between them, break them into two groups and ask them to line up on opposite walls).
- Each child places a yardstick against the wall near her feet.
- Invite the children to jump forward and then use the yardstick to measure how far they can jump. Repeat several times.
- Encourage the children to surpass their own previous jumps, but discourage competition among the children.

Read *How Much, How Many, How Far, How Heavy, How Long, How Tall Is 1000?* by Helen Nolan and illustrated by Tracy Walker.

How Long Is...?

This activity offers more measuring experience for the children. Even if they can't yet determine how many inches something is, they'll be proud to let you at least know something is "this long."

To Have

1 ruler, yardstick, or measuring tape per child

To Do

- Ask the children to use a ruler, yardstick, or measuring tape to measure the lengths of their legs.
- Once they've accomplished that task, other items to measure include the following:
  - shin (from knee to ankle)
  - pointer finger
  - pinky finger
  - foot
  - friend

More to Do

- Set the children free around the room to determine the length of any object they want to measure. They'll love the importance of this task. If you write down their findings, it will add even more value to their work.

Chapter 4

Basic Geometry

Among the expectations of the National Council of Teachers of Mathematics (NCTM) is that children in the preprimary grades be able to recognize and name two- and three-dimensional shapes, and that they be able to understand spatial relationships as the foundations of early geometry.

The space concepts listed in Principles and Standards for School Mathematics (NCTM, 2000) are as follows:

- **Position:** on/off, on top of/over/under, in/out, into/out of, top/bottom, above/below, in front of/in back of/behind, beside/by/next to, between
- **Direction:** up/down, forward/backward, around/through, to/from, toward/away from, sideways, across
- **Distance:** near/far, close to/far from
- **Organization and Pattern:** the arrangement of things to fit in a given space
- **Construction:** changing the size and shape of the space so things will fit

Many of these concepts lend themselves to exploration through physical experiences, so they are covered in the following activities. Also included in this chapter is an exploration of geometric shapes, beginning with lines and eventually encompassing points, angles, circles, squares, triangles, and rectangles.

HORIZONTAL

CIRCLE

DOWN

Introduces simple directions

Going Up

Up *and* down *are two of the simplest directional concepts. This activity allows the children to explore them in a fun way that also puts the children's imaginations to use.*

3RD FLOOR (UP)

GOING DOWN (2ND)

BOTTOM (1ST)

To Have

No materials needed

To Do

- Talk to the children about how elevators go up and down.
- Ask them to crouch down low, pretending to be elevators at the ground floor of a building.
- When you say "Going up!" they slowly rise. When you say "Going down!" they crouch down slowly. When you call out the number of a floor—for example, "Third floor!"—they pause in the process of either going up or down until receiving further direction from you.

Elevator Magic by Stuart J. Murphy (illustrated by G. Brian Karas) offers a fun look at elevators while also teaching subtraction.

Me & My Shadow

This partner activity reinforces the positional concepts of in front of *and* behind.

To Have

No materials needed

To Do

- One child stands with her back to the second child.
- The child in front performs various movements, both in place and traveling, and the child in back imitates the movements of, or "shadows," the child in front.
- At your signal, the children switch roles. Be sure to use the words *in front of* and *behind* in reference to where the children are standing.

More to Do

- Have the children play this game in threes, indicating that the middle child is *in between*.

Add to the children's understanding of shadows by reading *Moonbear's Shadow* by Frank Asch or *Shadows and Reflections* by Tana Hoban.

Reinforces spatial relationships

Over & Under

Over *and* under *relate to the spatial concept of position. However, because these words are also prepositions and opposites, this activity promotes emergent literacy as well as mathematical knowledge.*

To Have

A playground or small beach ball

To Do

- Stand in a circle with the children, with each child facing the back of the person to his or her right.
- Pass the ball backward *over* your head to the child behind you.
- Be sure to emphasize the word *over* when passing the ball. That child does the same, and the ball goes all the way around the circle in this manner.
- Next, everyone stands with their legs apart and passes the ball between their legs (*under* their bodies) to the person behind them.

More to Do

- When the children are comfortable with both of these ways of passing the ball, invite them to alternate between *over* and *under:* One child passes it *over* her head and the next child passes it *under* his body.

OVER

 *Over* and *under* are explored in Marthe Jocelyn's book, *Over Under.*

Linear Limbo

What more fun way to explore the concepts of under *and* horizontal lines *than by playing a game of limbo? This modified version allows the children to go under the rope in any way they wish! Also, using a long rope and slanting it makes it possible for several children to participate at once and to succeed at any level.*

To Have

A long rope

To Do

- Two children stand holding the ends of the rope, high enough to allow the children to walk under it. The rest of the children form a single-file line.
- Point out that both the rope and the children themselves are in straight lines.
- As each child takes a turn walking under the rope (be sure to emphasize the word *under*), she or he relieves one of the rope holders, who moves to the end of the line.
- After everyone has had a turn, the rope holders lower it slightly. When it becomes challenging for some of the children to get under it, the rope holders angle it, one child holding it at waist height and the other holding it as high as possible.
- The remaining children can go under it at any point and in any way they want.

More to Do

- Invite the children to try going over a slanted rope in any way they want, such as hopping, jumping, or leaping. **Safety Note:** Be sure to keep the rope low to the ground so that children do not trip over it.
- Use four children as rope holders, who create a circle with the rope. As each child moves under the rope, from the outside to the inside of the circle, he or she takes the place of a rope holder. You can also help the children create an oval, triangle, square, or rectangle under which the children "limbo."

Accompany this activity with *All-Time Favorite Dances* or Frank Leto's *Steel Band Jamboree.*

Reinforces spatial relationships

Over, Under, & More

Here's a second chance for the children to experience over *and* under. *This activity also promotes understanding of* around *and* through, *which are directional concepts.*

To Have

Materials for an obstacle course (cardboard boxes, jump ropes, plastic hoops, classroom furniture, and so on)
Display cards with illustrated and written directions

To Do

- Set up a simple obstacle course that includes, at each point, a card with a direction (both drawn and written) indicating which way the children should move: over, under, around, or through.
- Talk with the children about the positional words they will use in the obstacle course, and explain the cards to them.
- Read them through the course, explaining what to do as you go through it. For example, you might say, "Now we're going *under* the rope. Next, we'll go *through* the box."

More to Do

- Once the children are familiar with the course, make slight changes to it. For example, if the children were previously expected to go *under* a rope suspended between two pieces of furniture, try laying the rope flat and redirecting them to go *over* it.
- Place any object on the floor and invite the children to discover how many different ways they can move over or around it.
- If you have a low balance beam available, challenge the children to find two ways (or more) to move over it (for example: stepping, jumping, or slithering over it). How many ways can they find to move along it? (For example: scooting on the bottom, sliding on the tummy, walking, tiptoeing, or stepping sideways.)

Share *Over Under* by Marthe Jocelyn with the children.

To reinforce these concepts, sing and discuss songs such as "Ring Around the Rosie," "The Bear Went over the Mountain," She'll Be Comin' 'Round the Mountain," and "Over the River and Through the Woods."

Follow That Line

Geometric shapes begin with the simple line. This activity gives children the opportunity to explore a variety of lines that they can see and feel.

To Have

Posted drawings of vertical, horizontal, diagonal, crossed, curved, and crooked lines
Masking tape replicating the various types of lines on the floor
1 jump rope per child (optional)

To Do

- Invite the children to move along the pathways created by the various lines on the floor.

- Begin with simple locomotor skills, such as creeping and walking, and then change the skill every time the children complete one pass of all the lines. Other possible locomotor skills include jogging, jumping, galloping, hopping, and skipping (if the children are developmentally ready to do so).

More to Do

- Assign a different locomotor skill for each type of line. For example, straight lines are for walking, zigzagging lines are for galloping, and curving lines are for tiptoeing.
- When the children are ready for a greater challenge, instead of creating the lines yourself with masking tape, give the children jump ropes with which they can create their own lines. Once they create their lines, the children follow their paths using the locomotor skills of their choice.

Which Direction?

This activity provides additional practice with the spatial directions of up,
down, *and* sideways.

To Have

A large card with a large arrow printed on it

To Do

● Display the card so the arrow is pointed in one of four directions. If it is
pointing upward, the children stretch toward the ceiling. If it is pointing
downward, the children crouch down. If it is pointing either left or right, the
children take a step sideways in either of those directions.

UP   DOWN   RIGHT   LEFT

For a fun exploration of up and down, read *Up, Up, Down!* by Robert N. Munsch.

Above, Below, & On

The children explore three positional concepts in this activity.

To Have

1 jump rope per child

To Do

- Each child places his rope flat on the floor, in a straight horizontal line.
- Call out the words "above," "below," or "on," indicating where the children should stand in relation to the line.
- Call out the words in various orders and tempos!

More to Do

- If your group is small enough (and/or you have a long enough rope), you can do a similar activity with the children standing side by side. You will either have to secure the rope on both ends or assign two children to hold the ends. The rope should be waist high, with the children standing behind it. When you say, "above," the children reach their arms over the top of the rope. When you say, "below," they put their arms below the rope. And when you say, "on," they put their hands on the rope.

Share *Up Above and Down Below* by Sue Redding with the children.

Reinforces spatial relationships

Take Your Positions

This activity reinforces more challenging positional and directional concepts, as well as distance concepts. Again, because all of these concepts are also prepositions, this activity reinforces emergent literacy.

To Have

1 jump rope per child

To Do

● Each child places his or her rope on the floor. Invite the children to do the following:

- Stand beside the rope
- Stand with the rope behind him or her
- Stand with the rope in front of him or her
- Stand near the rope
- Stand far from the rope
- Walk throughout the room, around the ropes
- Walk toward the rope but then continue walking past it
- Walk toward the rope again
- Stand with the rope between the feet
- Stand on top of the rope
- Lie across the rope

Read *Under, Over, By the Clover: What Is a Preposition?* by Brian P. Cleary.

Silly Willy's Pre-Jump Rope Skills by Brenda Colgate gives children a variety of activities to do with ropes.

What's My Line?

This activity provides more opportunity for the children to experience lines. And because it contributes to the ability to replicate physically what the eyes see, it also falls under the content areas of art and emergent literacy (children need to replicate physically what they see in order to write).

To Have

Posted drawings of straight, crossed, curved, and crooked lines

To Do

- Discuss each of the lines with the children, assigning each its appropriate name (although you can't expect the children to recall them at this point).
- Invite them to replicate each with their bodies or with individual body parts.
- Name each as you point to it.

More to Do

- Divergent problem solving, in which there is more than one response to any single challenge, is vital to creative- and critical-thinking skills. You can give children the chance to experience divergent problem solving by encouraging them to "find another way." With this activity, for example, if a child demonstrates crossed lines with the arms and you present the challenge to find another way, the response might be crossed fingers.
- Call out the words "straight," "curving," and "crooked"—in various orders and at different tempos—challenging the children to match their body shapes with the word.
- Challenge the children to create the various lines with partners.
- Invite the children to find examples of the different lines throughout the room. Then ask them to show you with their bodies the kind of lines they find. For example, if they point out that a pencil lying down is a line, challenge them to show you the kind of line (straight) made by the pencil. If they point to the top of the wastebasket as a curved line, ask them to use their bodies to depict that kind of line.

Continues the exploration of lines

Which Way Does It Go?

This activity introduces the children to the concept of horizontal, vertical, and diagonal lines.

To Have

Posted pictures of the three kinds of lines, or a jump rope to be used for demonstration

To Do

- Show the children a vertical line and ask them to replicate it with their whole bodies. Can they make a vertical line with just one body part? Another?
- Repeat the process with horizontal and diagonal lines.

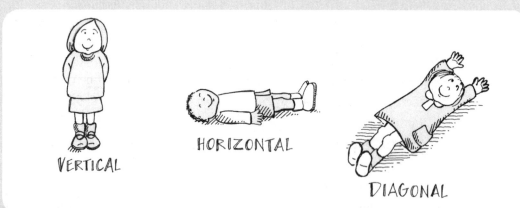

VERTICAL

HORIZONTAL

DIAGONAL

More to Do

- Invite the children to "paint" the different kinds of lines in the air in front of them, first with their hands and then with other body parts. Can they use their feet to paint them on the floor?

Read Mem Fox's *The Straight Line Wonder* to the children. What kind of line does the little boy create?

I Spy

Once the children have had ample experience with various kinds of lines, ask them to find some on their own.

To Have

No materials needed

To Do

- Chant "I spy with my little eye a line that is curving [a diagonal line, a vertical line, a line that is crooked, and so on]."
- The children then look around the room or playground, move to whatever they believe it might be (it's best if there's more than one possibility) and take on the shape of the chosen object.

CROOKED

STRAIGHT

Jean Marzollo and Walter Wick have created a number of wonderful *I Spy* books.

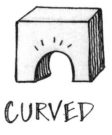

ROUND

SQUARE

CURVED

Basic Geometry   81

On the Path to Geometry

This activity provides additional experience with straight, curving, and zigzagging lines. However, because the children cannot actually see the lines they are creating, it is more abstract. That makes it both more challenging and less intimidating.

To Have

No materials needed

To Do

- Play a brief game of Follow the Leader, in which you move in straight, curving, and zigzagging pathways, pointing out each as the children experience them.
- Invite the children to go their own ways, walking first in straight lines, then in curving lines, and finally in zigzagging lines around the room. Follow the same pattern with other locomotor skills.

More to Do

- A more difficult challenge is to ask the children to move along straight, curving, and zigzagging pathways in sideward and backward directions.

Shrinking Room

Among the space concepts important to geometry are organization *and* pattern—*arranging things so they fit in a given space. With this game, it is the children who have to arrange themselves to fit in the assigned space—a space that gradually reduces!*

To Have

1 hoop per child

To Do

- Ask each child to step inside a hoop, pick it up, and put it around her or his waist.
- Challenge the children to imagine they are each inside either giant bubbles or cars on the highway (whichever image you think will work best with your group).
- Tell them to move around the room without touching anyone else's bubble or car. Stand with your arms out to your sides, acting as a "wall," beyond which they can't pass.
- Gradually, begin reducing the size of the area in which the children have to move.
- Be sure to stop while the children are still able to move around without touching another person's hoop! (If you don't have hoops, the children can still play this game by extending their arms out to their sides. Instead of avoiding contact with other hoops, they'll be avoiding contact with other hands.)

Come to Me

When the children have had ample experience with both personal space and the three types of pathways, they'll be ready for this game.

To Have

1 carpet square, hoop, or other type of "place marker" per child

To Do

- The children stand scattered throughout the room, each on or in the item marking his or her personal space.
- Stand in the center of the room where everyone can easily see you and instruct the children to come to you in a variety of ways. For example, you might say, "Come to me, traveling in a straight line."
- Once they reach you, give them directions for returning to their personal spaces; for example, "Return to your personal space in a curving line."

More to Do

- Incorporate directions (backward, sideward, and varying levels such as on tiptoe or near the floor) into your instructions.
- When the children are ready for a greater challenge, combine two instructions. For example, you might invite them to come to you "moving backward in a straight line."

To the Point

Points are part of early geometry, too. This activity introduces the children to the concept.

To Have

Miscellaneous items typically found in a classroom

To Do

- Show the children examples of different points found throughout the room (for example, the point of a pencil, the corner of a desk or book, the point of a clock hand).
- Now invite them to point their fingers and then their toes. Can they create a pointed shape with more than one finger? Invite the children to create pointed shapes with their arms, hands, feet, and whole bodies.

More to Do

- Challenge the children to create pointed shapes in pairs and trios.

Follow That Shape

This is similar to Follow That Line, only this time the children will travel along the three simple geometric shapes you create on the floor.

To Have

Posted pictures of circles, triangles, and squares

Masking tape

1 jump rope per child (optional)

To Do

- With the masking tape, create circles, triangles, and squares on the floor.
- Invite the children to move along pathways created by the various shapes, naming each for them.
- Begin with simple locomotor skills, such as creeping and walking, and then change the skill every time the children complete one pass of all the shapes. Other possible locomotor skills include jogging, jumping, galloping, hopping, and skipping (if the children are developmentally ready to do so).

More to Do

- Assign a different traveling skill for each shape. For example, squares are for walking, circles are for jogging, and triangles are for tiptoeing.
- When the children are ready for a greater challenge, instead of creating the shapes yourself with masking tape, give each child a jump rope with which to create their own shapes. Once each shape is made, the children follow its path with the locomotor skills of their choice.

The children have explored lines already, but they may not have made the connection between lines and geometric shapes. Point out that a circle is one continuous, curving line; a triangle is made up of three lines that join at three points; and a square consists of four connected lines, two horizontal and two vertical. Then share *When a Line Bends… A Shape Begins*, written by Rhonda Gowler Greene and illustrated by James Kaczman.

Getting in Shape

This activity continues the exploration of six of the geometric shapes developmentally appropriate for young children to discover.

To Have

Posted drawings of a circle, square, triangle, diamond, rectangle, and oval

To Do

- Discuss each of the shapes with the children, assigning each its appropriate name.
- Invite them to replicate each shape with their bodies or with individual body parts, one at a time (once again naming them as you point to them).

More to Do

- Encourage the children to "find another way" to make each shape.
- Challenge the children to create the various shapes with partners.
- Invite the children to find examples of the different shapes throughout the room. Then present challenges such as, "Show me the kind of shape made by a desktop."

A wonderful book about shapes is *First Shape Book* by Patti Barber and Ann Montague-Smith.

Included on Hap Palmer's *Learning Basic Skills, Volume 2* (available as part of the *Hap Palmer Learning Basic Skills Set)* are two songs appropriate for this activity: "Triangle, Circle or Square" and "One Shape, Three Shapes."

Reinforces awareness of geometric shapes

I Spy II

Once the children have had enough experience identifying various shapes, they are ready to find them on their own.

To Have

No materials needed

To Do

- Chant "I spy with my little eye a square (circle, triangle, and so on)." The children look around the room or playground and then move to whatever they've discovered that's in the shape you've called out (it is best if more than one possibility exists).
- Invite the children to take on the shapes of the chosen objects with their bodies or body parts. For example, if you "spy" something rectangular, some children might move to your desk and turn themselves into desk shapes.

Share *The Shape of Things,* written by Dayle Ann Dodds and illustrated by Julie Lacome, or *Shapes, Shapes, Shapes* by Tana Hoban with the children.

Making Shapes Together

This activity offers children a chance to experience geometric shapes in groups of three, making it a cooperative (social studies) activity as well as a mathematical one.

To Have

Pictures of a circle, triangle, square, and rectangle (optional)

To Do

- Divide the children into groups of three.
- Challenge each trio to work as a group to create various geometric shapes, such as a circle, triangle, square, and rectangle, using either their bodies as a whole or their body parts.
- Invite the children to think of new shapes they can create together. Can they make a diamond?
- Are there other shapes in the room that they can try to make?

More to Do

- Encourage the children to work in pairs and groups of four. What can they do with four people that they can't do with two? What is the perfect shape for three people? What are the problems that the children encounter when they work in pairs? Discuss their experiences.

Tana Hoban has created three books appropriate for this activity: *So Many Circles, So Many Squares;* and *Cubes, Cones, Cylinders & Spheres.*

Matching Shapes

This game gives children an opportunity to revisit some of the shapes they have learned, or to create shapes of their own. Because it involves cooperating and physically replicating what the eyes see, it also promotes learning in the areas of social studies, language arts, and art.

To Have

No materials needed

To Do

- Children choose partners and determine who is "A" and who is "B."
- At a signal from you, A moves to a different part of the room and creates a body shape of his choosing.
- He holds this position until B joins him and, facing him, assumes the same shape (like a mirror image).
- Once they do this, B forms a different shape, which A must match.

Now It's Symmetrical...
Now It's Not

The children may not yet be ready to fully understand the terms symmetrical *and* asymmetrical, *but they still can have fun experiencing the concepts!*

To Have

Examples of symmetrical and asymmetrical shapes

To Do

- Using your examples, point out that a symmetrical shape looks exactly the same on both sides and an asymmetrical shape does not.
- Show the children a symmetrical body shape—for example, standing with feet apart and arms out to sides.
- Once the children replicate it, make a simple movement that changes your position to create an asymmetrical shape—for example, raising one arm so it points toward the ceiling.
- Explain what you've done, and ask the children to replicate it once again.
- Continue in this manner, making easy symmetrical shapes and then simple movements that change them to asymmetrical.

More to Do

- Once the children are familiar with this concept, you can challenge them to perform this activity without your demonstrations.
- Eventually the children can try creating symmetrical shapes in pairs (for example, standing side by side with feet apart, inside hands linked, and arms out to sides). One partner then does something to create an asymmetrical shape (for example, lowering her outside arm).

Reinforces understanding of geometric shapes

Changing Shapes

Children may be able to see the differences between a circle and an oval, a square and a rectangle, and a square and a diamond, but they probably cannot determine what those differences are. This activity gives them an opportunity to explore and discover.

To Have

Posted side-by-side pictures of a circle and an oval, a square and a rectangle, and a square and a diamond

To Do

- Talk with the children about the difference between a circle and an oval.
- Ask them to show you the former with the whole body or with body parts. How can they change what they have done to create an oval? Repeat this exercise with the two remaining sets of shapes.

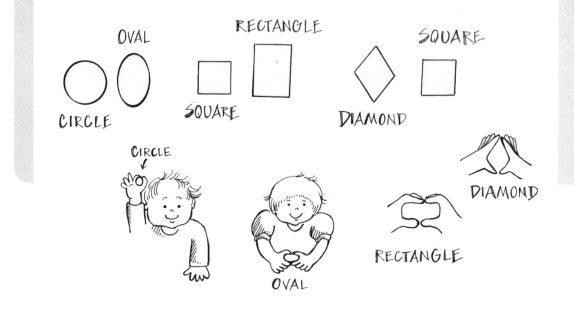

What's Your Angle?

Angles are made of two connecting lines, and squares, rectangles, triangles, and diamonds all have them. The human body has them, too!

To Have

Posted pictures of squares, rectangles, triangle, diamonds, and angles alone

To Do

- Explain angles to the children, identifying them on the posted pictures.
- Point out the natural angles made by the arms and shoulders and the legs and feet on the human body.
- Invite the children to find other ways they can make angles with their bodies and body parts.

More to Do

- Challenge the children to create angles with partners.

DIAMOND

RECTANGLE

Chapter 5

Sequencing & Patterning

Children are introduced to sequencing when they begin to count from 1–10. But it is only after they understand one-to-one correspondence that the concept begins to have meaning for them. This section starts with the children simply counting off in sequence and continues with activities that require the children to perform movements in sequence. When every other child is asked to do something different, we begin our introduction to patterning, which Copley (2000) tells us is "the science and language" of mathematics. She notes, "Because the study of patterns is basic to all mathematical thinking, it has a close natural connection to the other math content areas."

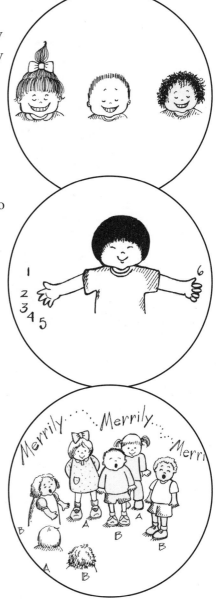

Count Off

This simple introduction to sequencing begins with the children counting off. If you have a large group, divide the children into two groups with each group starting at number one. This will reduce the time children spend waiting.

To Have

No materials needed

To Do

- The children stand side by side and count off sequentially. If necessary, you can begin by pointing to each child in turn and calling out the number yourself.

More to Do

- Once the children are familiar with the concept, invite them to take a step forward as they each say their numbers.
- When the end of the line is reached, the children can reverse the process, beginning the count at that end.
- Have the children count forward from one to the end of the line and then reverse the process, counting backward.

Counting Fingers

This activity, which reinforces counting and sequencing skills, may require a lot of repetition, but opening and closing fingers one at a time has the added bonus of improving hand strength and fine-motor coordination.

To Have

No materials needed

To Do

- Have the children curl their hands into loose fists.
- Then, as you count (very slowly at first) from 1–10, they uncurl one finger at a time.
- Reverse the process, counting from 10–1, with the children curling one finger at a time back into the palms of their hands.

C. W. Bowie's *Busy Fingers*, illustrated by Fred Willingham, offers a look at the different ways that fingers move. Counting on fingers is included!

Reinforces sequencing skills

This Is My Friend

This is one of my favorite games because it's so friendly. Not only does it offer practice with sequencing, but it also creates a feeling of welcome and belonging.

To Have

No materials needed

To Do

- Stand in a circle with the children, with everyone holding hands.
- Raise the hand of the child to your right or left, saying, "This is my friend, _____." That child says her name and raises the arm of the next child in the circle, saying, "This is my friend, _____."
- The process continues all the way around the circle until all of the children have had a chance to say their names and all arms are in the air. The group then takes a big bow!

More to Do

- Once the children know the names of their classmates, they can introduce each other instead of themselves. For example, Keith might raise the arm of the child to his left and say, "This is my friend, Rachel."
- When the children are familiar with one another, they can add something of interest about the person they're introducing. For example, Keith might say, "This is my friend Rachel, and she likes music."

Pass a Face

Children are genetically programmed to learn through imitation. This fun activity uses imitation to help children learn about sequencing because the movement is sequential around the circle. Also, because the face remains the same all the way around, there's an element of patterning to this activity, as well.

To Have

No materials needed

To Do

- Sit with the children in a circle and begin by making a face that each child must take turns imitating until it comes back to you.
- Once it does, you can make a different face and get it going in the other direction.
- When the children are ready, let them take turns choosing a face to pass around.

Roberta Grobel Intrater has created a series of board books called *Baby Faces* that are great for sharing with the children either before or after this activity.

Reinforces sequencing skills

Pass a Movement

This activity uses the same principle as Pass a Face, but because it involves the whole body, it's a more challenging way to explore sequence.

To Have

No materials needed

To Do

- Stand in a circle with the children and perform a simple action (for example, hopping, twirling, or bending and straightening the knees).
- The child to your left or right, depending on which direction you've decided to go, performs the same action, and so on all the way around the circle. It should look just the same when it gets back to you!
- Start again with a new action or, if the children are ready to handle the responsibility, let them take turns beginning the process.

HOP

TWIRL

Pass It On

In addition to reinforcing the concept of sequencing, Pass It On helps improve eye-hand coordination and cooperative skills.

To Have

1 beanbag or small ball

To Do

- The children stand in a circle.
- One child holds the beanbag and passes it to the child either to his right or left.
- The process continues all the way around the circle until the beanbag is back in the last child's hands. That child then passes the beanbag in the opposite direction.

More to Do

- An alternative is to count consecutively as the children pass the beanbag from one child to the next. For example, the first child to hold the beanbag says "one." The second child to receive it says "two," and so forth around the circle.
- Have the children form two lines facing each other and standing less than 12" apart. Challenge them to toss the beanbag gently back and forth, zigzagging down the lines. Point out the zigzagging pattern to the children.

Introduces patterns

Echo

This introduction to musical meters (beat groupings) is also an experience in patterning, but the children will think it is just a fun game.

To Have

Rhythm sticks (optional)

To Do

- Clap and count out a small group of beats (for example, 1-2 or 1-2-3) and then ask the children to echo what you did.
- Repeat several times, sometimes using the same beat groups and sometimes varying them.

More to Do

- Using rhythm sticks instead of hands can add color and fun to the activity.
- To make the game more challenging, clap without counting aloud.
- When the children are ready, you can combine beat groupings. For example, you might beat out 1-2, 1-2-3. Repeat these several times.

You can complement this activity with *Little Beaver and the Echo* by Amy MacDonald, with illustrations by Sarah Fox-Davies.

Many songs on Hap Palmer's *The Feel of Music* explore echoing.

Pass a Rhythm

This game is like Pass a Movement or the game of Gossip except that a beat is passed around the circle instead of a movement or a word. In addition to reinforcing sequencing and patterning, this game also fosters active listening and a sense of rhythm, both essential to emergent literacy.

To Have

Rhythm sticks (optional)

To Do

- Sit in a circle with the children and beat out a simple rhythm (for example, 1-2) with claps on your lap or on the floor in front of you. (Counting the beats aloud at first can help the children succeed.)
- The child next to you repeats that rhythm, and the game continues in a similar manner around the circle.
- Start the game again with a different rhythm (for example, 1-2-3).

More to Do

- Using rhythm sticks instead of hands can add color and fun to the activity.
- When the children are ready to move on to something more challenging, you can combine rhythms. For example, you might beat out 1-2, 1-2-3.
- Eventually the children can take turns choosing rhythms.

 Share Ella Jenkins's *Adventures in Rhythm* with the children.

The Wave

When fans at a sporting event perform the wave, it's the perfect example of sequencing in motion. When the children have a chance to do it they will be thinking more about feeling grownup than about sequence, but that's okay!

To Have

No materials needed

To Do

- Ask the children if they have ever seen spectators do the wave at a sporting event.
- Demonstrate the movement used to do a wave at a sporting event and explain that when people do the same movement, one immediately following the other (in sequence), it looks like a wave in the ocean.
- With the children standing side by side, encourage them to perform the wave. If necessary at first, you can start at one end and move to the other end, pointing at each child, one after another.
- The children, in turn, lift their arms into the air.
- Once the children have successfully performed the wave going in one direction, encourage them to try it in the other direction, or with a different movement.

Every Other

This game is also like Pass a Movement, but it focuses on patterning and requires the children to pay even closer attention.

To Have

No materials needed

To Do

- The children stand in a circle. One child performs a simple action (for example, clapping twice). The next child chooses a *different* action (for example, stomping twice). The third child repeats the first child's action, and the fourth child repeats the action of the second.

- The process continues in this manner all the way around the circle.

Reinforces understanding of patterning

Circle Design

Children will be better able to see and understand patterns when they create the patterns themselves. This activity allows them to do just that.

To Have

No materials needed

To Do

- The children stand in a circle with their hands on the shoulders of the children on either side of them.
- Point out that the pattern of the circle is uniform—the same—all the way around because all of the children are standing in the same way.
- Now help every other child to place a foot inside the circle. The pattern has been changed, but it is still uniform.
- Help the children brainstorm other ways they can change the pattern. (For example, alternate children can either bend at the knees or stand on tiptoe.) Can they find a design that isn't uniform? (For example, every child assumes a different pose.)

Row, Row, Row Your Boat

This old favorite is in an AB form. The first section—"Row, row, row your boat gently down the stream"—is A. "Merrily, merrily, merrily, merrily; life is but a dream" is B. When the children perform a simple movement to each section, the pattern reveals itself.

To Have

No materials needed

To Do

- The children stand in a circle.
- Designate alternate children to be either A or B (that is, the first child is A, the second is B, and so forth).
- As the children sing the song, those designated as A step forward during their section, returning to their places after the word "stream."
- The children designated as B then step forward as they sing their lyrics, stepping back after "dream."
- This may take some practice, and you may have to orchestrate it at first; but the children will still enjoy it.

More to Do

- The children stand in two single-file lines—As and Bs. As the children in the A section sing, they begin to move forward, pretending to row a boat. They freeze in place at the conclusion of their section, at which point the children in the B section sing and "row." Continue in this manner across the room—and back, if you like. (Be sure the children don't make a contest out of this to see who can reach the other side of the room first, as the pattern will be deemed inconsequential to the competition.)

Read *Row, Row, Row Your Boat* by Iza Trapani.

"Row, Row, Row Your Boat" is one of the songs on *Rhythms of Childhood* by Ella Jenkins.

Sequencing & Patterning   107

Promotes understanding of sequencing

Step, Step, Jump

Performing a sequence of movements helps children better understand the concept of sequencing. And when they create their own sequences, they take ownership of them, thus making the idea of sequencing more appealing. Also, because linking movements to create sequences isn't all that different from linking words to form phrases and sentences, this activity contributes to emergent literacy as well as to math skills.

To Have

No materials needed

To Do

- Demonstrate what it looks like to step, step, and jump.
- Invite the children to imitate you, saying aloud the words "step, step, jump" to help them.
- Repeat this several times.
- When they have experienced success with this, invite them to create their own sequence of steps and jumps—using as many of each as they wish.

More to Do

- Invite the children to combine any two or three locomotor and/or nonlocomotor skills, in any order and as many of each as they want. Possible combinations include the following:
  - Jump, turn
  - Jump, stretch
  - Jump, stretch, turn
  - Run, leap
  - Run, leap, sway
  - Hop, swing
  - Hop, swing, stretch

1-2-3-4

This experience with counting, clapping, stepping, and resting is a patterning exercise in disguise!

To Have

No materials needed

To Do

Because some children are visual as opposed to auditory learners, you can help all of the children achieve success with this activity if you initially perform it with them. Start slowly, performing the following actions:

- Count to four.
- Take four steps.
- Take three steps and clap once.
- Take two steps and claps twice.
- Take one step and clap three times.

More to Do

- Reverse the previous order and pick up the tempo a bit.
- Challenge the children to perform the following:
  - Count to four.
  - Clap four times.
  - Take four steps (in place).
  - Rest to the count of four (they can put their hands to their cheeks, as though napping).
  - Count to two; clap twice.
  - Clap twice; take two steps.
  - Take two steps; rest two counts.
  - Count to one; clap three times.
  - Clap once; take three steps.
  - Take one step; rest three counts.
  - Count to three; clap once.
  - Clap three times; take one step.
  - Take three steps; rest one count.

You can find a musical version of the activity described in the More to Do section of Rae Pica's *Moving & Learning Series: Early Elementary Children.*

Chapter 6

Simple Computation

Addition and subtraction are also known as *change operations,* *arithmetic,* or simply *adding to* and *taking away.* Before children can perform these operations mentally, they must experience them physically. Typically, that involves such tactile experiences as counting while touching objects and then removing or adding to the objects. Here, it involves removing or adding children or body parts! After many such activities, we will introduce some simple division.

Unlike other classroom activities that may or may not enable you to determine which children are having trouble with these concepts, the experiences suggested here provide ample opportunity for authentic assessment.

Introduces subtraction

Three Little Monkeys

*The children will think they are simply getting a chance to jump, but they will
also be practicing subtraction.*

To Have

No materials needed

To Do

- Divide the children into groups of three and assign each child within the group a number from one to three.
- Read aloud the nursery rhyme below, inviting the children to jump to its rhythm. Each time the rhyme indicates that a monkey has fallen off the bed, one child separates him- or herself from the other "monkeys" (but can continue jumping so there's constant participation).
- On the last line of the last verse, the three children in each group can move back to the "bed" (the spot in which they began the activity) and lie down.

Three little monkeys
Jumping on the bed,
One fell off and bumped his head.
Mother called the doctor and the doctor said,
"No more monkeys jumping on the bed."
Two little monkeys…

One little monkey
Jumping on the bed,
One fell off and bumped his head.
Mother called the doctor and the doctor said,
"Get those monkeys back to bed."

More to Do

- When the children are ready for greater challenges, change the rhyme to four or five little monkeys.

Five Little Monkeys Jumping on the Bed, by Eileen Christelow, is the perfect accompaniment to this activity.

"Three Little Monkeys" can be found on Maryann "Mar" Harman's *Playing and Learning With Music*.

Plus & Minus

This simple activity offers experience with both counting and simple computation.

To Have

Nothing needed

To Do

- Invite the children to sit in a circle on the floor.
- When you call out a child's name, that child gets up and stands in the center of the circle.
- Ask the children how many are in the center. When they've answered, call out another child's name. That child joins the child already in the center. Ask the children how many are in the circle now.
- Continue like this until you've asked as many children as you want into the center, asking the group each time to tell you how many are there.
- Then begin subtracting the children one at a time!

More to Do

- When the children are ready for a greater challenge, add or subtract two or three children at a time.

Alan Stern's *Sing a Sum… or a Remainder* offers basic addition and subtraction songs.

Roll Over

Acting out this popular song helps children hear, see, and feel simple subtraction!

To Have

Recording of "Roll Over" (optional)

To Do

- Have the children lie on the floor, side by side, pretending they are in a big bed.
- Then, as you and the children sing the following song, they all roll over on the fourth line, with one child rolling further than the others on the fifth line of each verse sung.
- Begin the song with a number equal to the number of children playing.

*There were [10] in the bed,
And the little one said,
"Roll over, roll over."
So they all rolled over,
And one fell out.*

There were [nine] in the bed...

*There was one in the bed,
And the little one said,
"Alone at last!"*

Precede or follow this activity with Merle Peek's *Roll Over: A Counting Book*!

The song is available on *Get Ready, Get Set, Sing* by Sarah Barchas.

Add 'Em & Subtract 'Em

Fingers have always been the perfect tools for mathematical calculations. Here the children will use them to make addition and subtraction less abstract.

To Have

No materials needed

To Do

- Ask the children to hold up the fingers on one hand and to count on them from one to five.
- Invite them to fold in the thumb and to count the remaining fingers. Explain that they've subtracted one from five to get four.
- Continue in this manner, subtracting and adding fingers.

More to Do

- Eventually the children can use the fingers on both hands. Before adding and subtracting, however, they should hold their hands side by side and tell you how many fingers they have on each hand. Use this to explain the concept of *equal*.

 Simple addition and subtraction are among the concepts included in *Dancing Numerals* by Rosemary Hallum and Henry "Buzz" Glass.

Promotes understanding of subtraction

How Many Children Standing at the Wall?

This activity subtracts one child at a time and makes an excellent transition activity when you're moving from group to free time.

To Have

No materials needed

To Do

- Arrange the children along a wall in a side-by-side line.
- Beginning with the number of children in the group, sing the following to the tune of "99 Bottles of Pop on the Wall."
- Point to each child who is to exit, assigning them randomly.

[15] *children standing at the wall,*
[15] *children at the wall.*
One moves away and goes off to play.
[14] *children*
standing at the wall.

- Repeat until there are no children at the wall!

Hap Palmer's *Math Readiness* teaches concepts and vocabulary needed for an understanding of basic mathematics.

Bottle Bowling

You can use this modified version of an adult game to provide children practice with subtraction. As a bonus, it also helps develop eye-hand coordination.

To Have

Several large, empty soda bottles per child
1 large playground ball or small beach ball per child

To Do

- Arrange the bottles in close proximity, asking the children to count how many there are.
- One child stands at a short distance from the bottles (at whatever distance feels comfortable) and rolls the ball toward the bottles.
- Together, count the bottles knocked down, explaining that you've begun with one number of bottles but have now subtracted some (cite the number).
- Count the standing bottles; this is what's left. The child then returns to the starting point and rolls the ball again.
- Continue this process until all of the bottles have been knocked down.
- Once they have been, stand them up and repeat the process!

How Many Parts Now?

This activity begins with counting but becomes an exercise in simple addition and subtraction.

To Have

No materials needed

To Do

- Invite the children to place a certain number of body parts on the floor. (If you've asked them to put five parts on the floor, there should only be five parts—for example, two hands, two knees, and one foot—touching the floor.)
- Once they've done this, ask them to *subtract* one part. How many are left?
- If they *add* two parts, how many are touching?
- Continue in this manner, encouraging them to vary the body parts used and asking them to tell you how many parts are touching the floor after each challenge to add or subtract.

The Doorbell Rang, by Pat Hutchins, offers lessons in simple computation.

Numbers in Motion

Try this exercise in addition when the children are becoming more adept at both counting and cooperation.

To Have

Recording for children to move to
CD or tape player

To Do

- Invite the children to move in any way they wish while the music is playing.
- When it stops, you call out a number, and the children get together with enough children to make up that number, connecting in some way.
- When the music begins again, the groups of children move together to the music.
- For example, if you call out "three," each child gets together with two more children, linking hands or elbows, and then moving as a group of three until the music stops again and you call out a different number.

 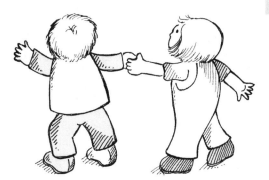

Ray Gibson's *Fun with Numbers* involves counting, adding, subtracting, and sharing.

Divvy Them Up

This elementary lesson in division is also an excellent way to arrange children into two or three groups without any of the hassle of "choosing sides."

To Have

No materials needed

To Do

- The children stand in a side-by-side or single-file line and count off into two groups by saying either "one" or "two." (If necessary, you can assist them by pointing to consecutive children and counting off yourself.)
- The "ones" go to one side of the room and the "twos" to the other side.
- Explain to the children that they've just been divided in half.

More to Do

- Instead of going to different sides of the room, the two groups can form concentric circles, making this also a lesson in geometry.
- Count off in threes, with each of the three groups then going to different parts of the room. Explain that the group has been divided by three.
- Arrange all the children in a side-by-side line. Before dividing them into two groups, ask the children to remember who is standing on either side of them. Once the children have counted off and are on opposite sides of the room, ask them to walk toward the center and to come back together so they're in their original positions (for example, they should be once again standing with the same children on either side of them).

Subtracting Steps

In Step Forward in Chapter 3, the children were required to first recognize a number and then to count it in steps forward. This game uses the same premise but also becomes an exercise in subtraction as the children are asked to recognize a number and to take that many steps backward.

To Have

The numbers 1–10 on individual cards

To Do

- The children line up side by side at one end of the room.
- Stand facing them at the opposite end and hold up one of the cards for them to see (it's best to start with low numbers).
- The children then take that number of steps toward you, counting aloud as they walk.
- At random times, before holding up a card, you say, "Now subtract…" This indicates the number of steps they should take in a backward direction (subtracting from their forward progress). Again, you should begin with low numbers.

More to Do

- When the children are developmentally ready, you can ask them to tell you the number resulting from their actions. For example, if they've taken five steps forward and then two backward, you can ask them what the result of five minus two is.
- To give the children an opportunity to practice different locomotor skills, replace the steps with jumps or hops. (Other locomotor skills may be too challenging to perform in a backward direction.)

 Alan Stern's *Sing a Sum… or a Remainder* teaches basic addition and subtraction facts.

Reinforces awareness of operations symbols

Sign Me Up

The plus and minus signs, like most of computation, can be very abstract to young children. This simple activity can help children better understand the purpose of these signs.

To Have

Plus and minus signs, posted

To Do

- Demonstrating for the children, ask them to place a forearm horizontally in front of the chest.
- Then ask the children to place the other forearm vertically at the halfway point of the first forearm, creating a plus sign.
- Point to your posted plus sign and explain to the children that when they put two things together, they're adding.
- Ask the children to move their vertical arm, leaving only the "minus sign."
- Point to your posted minus sign, explaining that when they take something away, they're subtracting. Repeat several times.

For children six years and older, "Plus Minus Boogie" is just one of the math-related songs on Rock 'n Learn's *Addition/Subtraction Country*. If you prefer rock to country music, you can find "Plus Minus Jam" on *Addition/Subtraction Rock*.

References

Copley, J.V. (2000). *The young child and mathematics.* Washington, DC: National Association for the Education of Young Children.

Charlesworth, R., & Lind, K.K. (2002). *Math and science for young children.* Clifton Park, NY: Delmar Learning.

Essa, E. (2003). *Introduction to early childhood education.* Clifton Park, NY: Delmar Learning.

Fauth, B. (1990). Linking the visual arts with drama, movement, and dance for the young child. In W.J. Stinson (Ed.), *Moving and learning for the young child* (pp. 159-187). Reston, VA: AAHPERD.

Gardner, H. (1993). *Frames of mind: The theory of multiple intelligences.* New York: Basic Books.

Jensen, E. (2000). *Learning with the body in mind: The scientific basis for energizers, movement, play, games, and physical education.* Thousand Oaks, CA: Corwin Press.

Mayesky, M. (2002). *Creative activities for young children.* Clifton Park, NY: Delmar Learning.

National Council of Teachers of Mathematics (NCTM). (2000). *Curriculum and evaluation standards for school mathematics.* Reston, VA: Author.

Orlick, T. (1982). *The second cooperative sports & games book: Over 200 noncompetitive games for kids and adults both.* New York: Pantheon Books.

Pica, R. (2001). *Wiggle, giggle, & shake: 200 ways to move & learn.* Beltsville, MD: Gryphon House.

Pica, R. (2006). *Great games for young children: Over 100 games to develop self-confidence, problem-solving skills, and cooperation.* Beltsville, MD: Gryphon House.

Glossary

Asymmetrical shapes: Shapes in which the two sides of a central dividing line are dissimilar.

Change operations: Another name for addition and subtraction.

Computation: The process of calculating something, or of working out the answer to a mathematical problem.

Construction: Changing the size and shape of the space so things will fit.

Direction: Includes such spatial relationships as up/down; forward/backward; around/through; to/from; toward/away from; sideways; across

Distance: Includes such spatial relationships as near/far; close to/far from.

Equal: When groups of people or objects have the same amount in each.

Measurement: Assigning a number to things for purposes of comparison.

Number recognition: The identification of numerals.

One-to-one correspondence: The ability to match numbers to objects or object to object. For example: the numbers one to five matching five blocks, or matching one sock to one shoe.

Organization and Pattern: The arrangement of things to fit in a given space.

Patterning: Making or finding regularities.

Position: Includes such positional relationships as on/off; on top of/over/under; in/out; into/out of; top/bottom, above/below; in front of/in back of/behind; beside/by/next to; between

Quantitative concepts: Part of the language of mathematics, these ideas are related to that which is measurable.

Rote memorization: Reciting from memory.

Sequencing: Ordering events. For example, 1-2-3 is a counting sequence; hop-skip-jump is a movement sequence.

Spatial relationships: In geometry, refers to relative positions in space.

Symmetrical shapes: Shapes in which both sides of a central dividing line are identical.

Indexes

Index of Children's Books

Index

Jump into Literacy

Active Learning for Preschool Children

Rae Pica

Jump into Literacy combines children's love of active games with more than 100 lively literacy activities. Written by a well-known children's movement specialist, these joyful games will engage the whole child in moving and playing as well as a way to develop the literacy skills needed for reading and writing. Each activity is complete with a literacy objective, materials list, instructions, and extension activities. Most of the activities include suggestions for related music and children's books. 136 pages. 2007

Gryphon House | ISBN 978-0-87659-009-6 | 15462

Great Games for Young Children

Over 100 Games to Develop Self-Confidence, Problem-Solving Skills, and Cooperation

Rae Pica

Both new and classic games (with a non-competitive twist) that get everybody moving, laughing and learning! The games in this book benefit the whole child, addressing all three domains of child development: cognitive, social/emotional, and physical. You'll find everything you need to play more than 100 great games, including outside games, musical games, circle games, concept games, and cooperative games. 136 pages. 2006.

Gryphon House | ISBN 978-0-87659-006-5 | 11308

Wiggle, Giggle & Shake

200 Ways to Move and Learn

Rae Pica

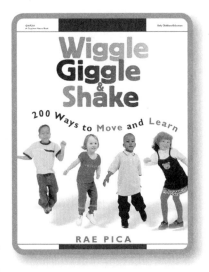

Enhance your classroom with 200 movement-inspiring activities for children ages 4–8. Explore 38 popular classroom themes such as holidays, nature, animals, nutrition, and more with simple, practical, and fun movement activities and ideas grouped according to these popular themes. The CD features 12 favorite songs from the book. 224 pages. 2001.

Gryphon House | ISBN 978-0-87659-244-1 | 19284

Educational Activities | 29431 | CD

Available at your favorite bookstore, school supply store, or order from Gryphon House at 800.638.0928 or www.gryphonhouse.com